# BARCELONA COLORING BOOK

---

## *Color Barcelona's Beautiful Attractions*

---

**ARTHUR BENJAMIN**

This page intentionally left blank.

# ABOUT THE BOOK

Barcelona is one of the world's most exciting places to visit for a reason. Explore the unique architectural beauty of Barcelona's most famous sights through this unique coloring book that includes Barcelona's most famous architectural and tourist attractions.

Printed in the United States of America
ISBN: 978-1619495456

# CONTENTS

This page intentionally left blank.

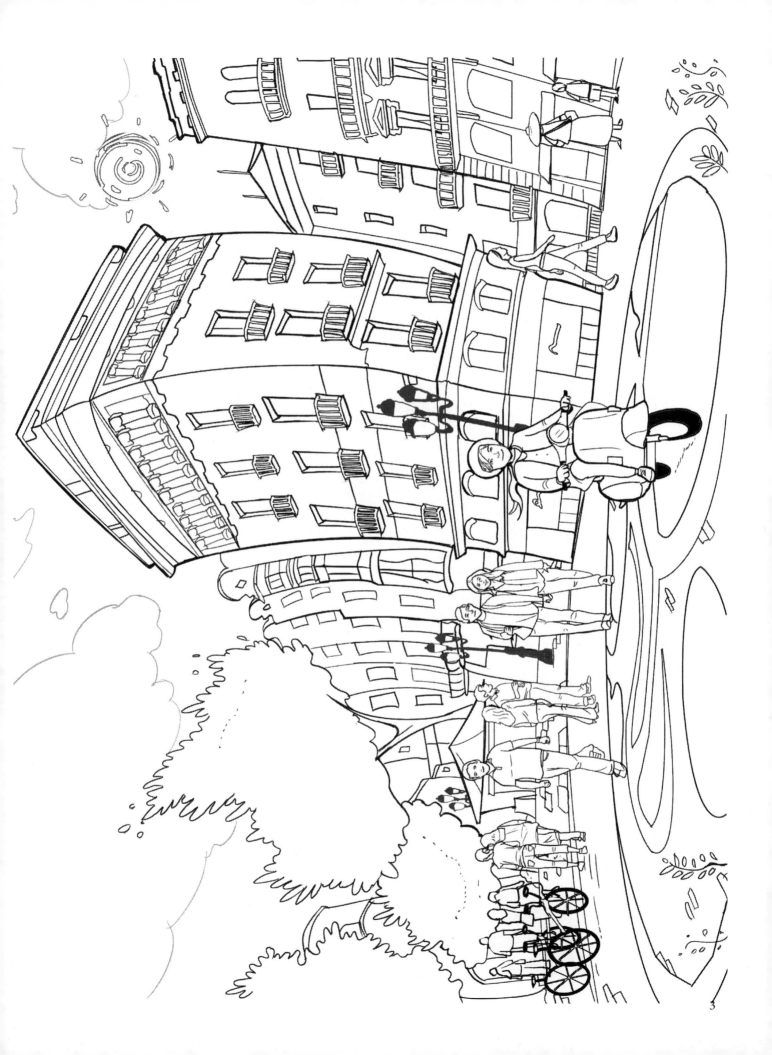

Plate 1.

Plate 2.

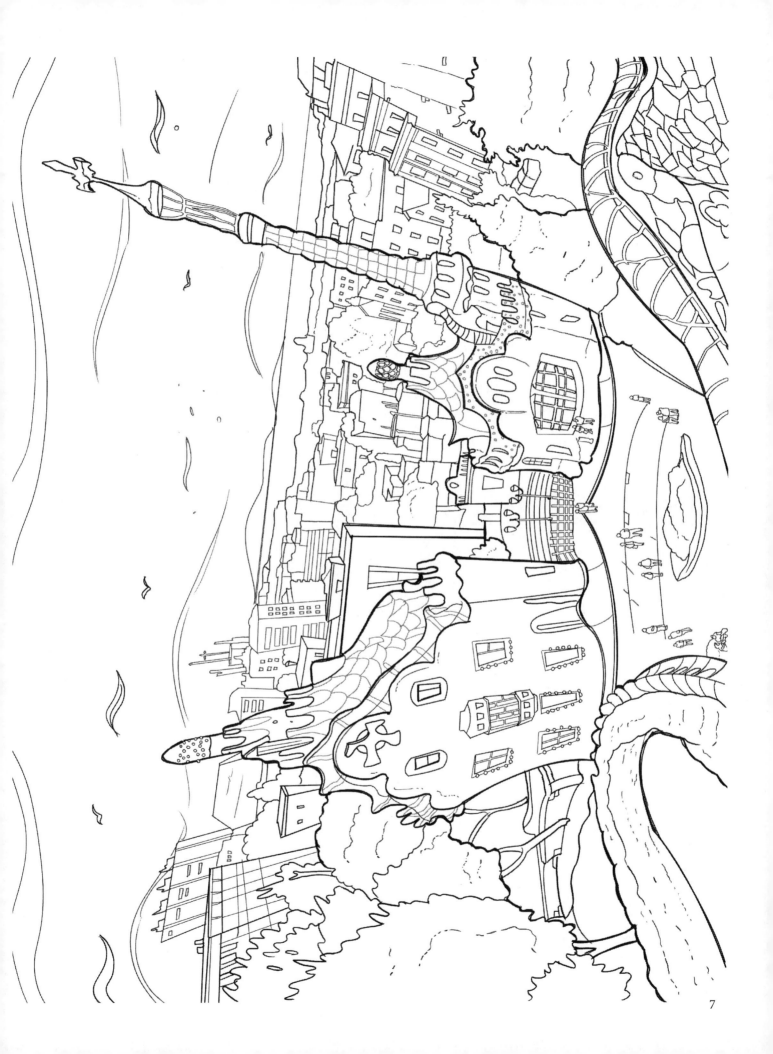

**Plate 3.**

**Plate 4.**

11

Plate 5.

13

Plate 6.

Plate 7.

17

**Plate 8.**

# ABOUT THE BOOK

Barcelona is one of the world's most exciting places to visit for a reason. Explore the unique architectural beauty of Barcelona's most famous sights through this unique coloring book that includes Barcelona's most famous architectural and tourist attractions.

This page intentionally left blank.

Made in the USA
Las Vegas, NV
08 July 2023